Sunfishing

Linda E. Chown
Editor: Abigail R. E. Best

Sunfishing

Author Contact: lindachown8@gmail.com

ISBN: 978-1-946671-19-6

Printed in the United States of America

My heart speaks before my words
stand out in the crowd
of windows and open mouths
my heart is my communist
my lone wolf my bride.

Linda Chown

To Buck always

Often times
the poem comes to mind obliquely,
as movement comes in water

Francis "Buck" Hosman

Introduction

Interview by Jamie Dades

JAMIE: I know you've been writing poetry for most of your life. How has your writing evolved?

LINDA: Initially, I wrote poetry feeling and being rather locked in, in the confines of McCarthyism and terrible asthma. These poems were outcries, full of a sense of being an outsider and a non-success. This first stage of my poetry was full of words, big words sometimes, as I was reading a lot of Faulkner at a young age. And I think my poems were without much nominal direction.

A second stage took place as I went to San Francisco State University and got a degree in Creative Writing. Then, I worked intimately with and heard truly great poets who encouraged me to write spare poems, to take off the loud pedals of my poetry piano. I wrote at this time very lean poetry, often of minute changes in the physical world, of bird calls, of colors blending. Sometimes, I also wrote at this time much longer narrative poems presenting moments of meeting, losing or finding. Then, there was a long time I lived and taught in Spain and the poetry stopped for some years, also when I went to get my Ph.D.

Now, in this third phase, I'm writing of unspoken traumas of artists in poems which I am calling *intrications.* As a result, I think my poetry has become freer and truer. I'm not now attempting to use strong fine words, but to allow language to match and measure the person I've become and am becoming. Also, now I write without immediate readers. That fact alone gives me a kind of freedom I didn't have before when people "made suggestions." My poems today draw upon the first period of Faulkneresque big word poems and the spare lean writing of my creative writing days. It's as though I can now write of anything in a form which has more hybrid, mingling poetic terseness and prose expansiveness within a guiding imagery.

JAMIE: Why is poetry important?

LINDA: Poetry refreshes who we are and opens our eyes. It is a second sight on all that we've known and done. It penetrates into the invisible world we don't speak of often and thus can bring us together. I heard many of the best poets reading in San Francisco and London. I was lucky enough to hear Voznesensky. Once, he said "metaphor is the motor of form." Tomas Tranströmer, a genius of internal life and artistic form, wrote: "We look almost happy out in the sun, while we bleed to death from wounds we don't know about.' Poetry is the biggest surprise. It can be our double, echo, enhance our solitudes, and tell us how the world is in its mysterious questioning. Poetry is a beautiful agent of radicalism in all ways.

Citations from interview

Chown, Linda. "An Interview with Poet Linda E. Chown & A Sampler of Her Poetry, Part 1." Jamie Dedes' The Poet by Day Webzine, December 20, 2018. https://jamiededes.com/2018/12/20/an-interview-with-poet-linda-a-sampler-of-her-poetry-part-1/.

Table of Contents

Personalities

Words

Places

Considerations

Moments

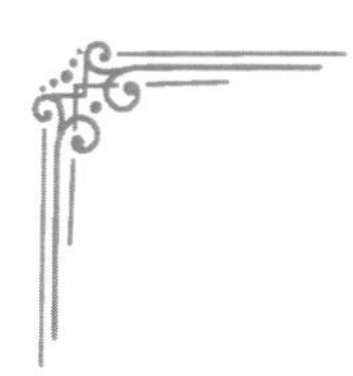

Personalities

People aren't meant to be perfect.
We're all imperfect people looking for perfect moments
to share with other imperfect people.

–Shaun Hutchinson

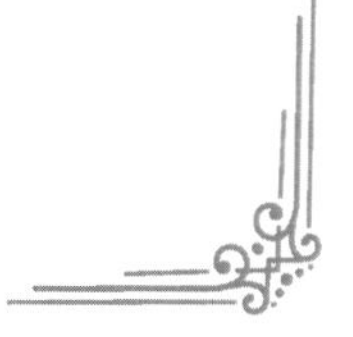

Intense Little Girl

She had an axe to
Grind with poor hearts.
She would burn and fester
Her hands when others went
Down to be like little threads of string
How she burned all asunder
So that her mind heaved hurt
And heart together until
Her small round red buttons swelled
Astray. She would not ever play little.

The past is always carried
into the present by small
things.
-Michael Ondaatje

Her Green Dress

Once my mother made a dress.
From the beginning she made it
With one of those store-bought
Jig-saw puzzle paper patterns.
It came out to be a stiff lime green
With severe shoulder pads.
Austere, just like the bun she wore
Which pulled her high cheek-boned face
Back just too far to see her through.
My mother had her way of making things,
Of finishing beginnings.
It was a way she had of hearing
Not just listening: it was a full court press hearing
Like a papal audience or gazing
Up at the stars awestruck
In Hayden Planetarium.
Hers was that padded touch hearing which remembered,
Which held on long past overtime,
Stitching seams to live in by.

to Oliver Sacks
for everything

When Seeing Beyond Yourself

you are just what you were then
when you used to stare at those fillies
flicking fly-thick tails
in a California twilight
your dark eyes spokes then
just as you are now trying to see
beyond yourself as we do
when we get blind and baffled

To My Father

That May Night in Statesboro, Georgia

Just get stronger I thought
& the word *hogtie* hits me big to say out.
I dream of a Georgia night inching on
In hard heat, long grass grasping
Our feet, intrusive. All I could do was cry,
Wetting my soup, dripping the clams.
Just get stronger I thought as he
Sank down into his long arms
Slithering off away far away.
Death sure was coming on him fast.
That black Georgia night done made us stall.
The blaring soul music made me bawl.
Ray Charles & Georgia got me
Baffled and bound in this quaint mourning mind.

Closet Poorness

Being closet poor and excluded
taught me
to like meatloaf and slippery onions,
to drink chocolate milk on the side,
taught me gender before the word
became the fashion.
My straining intellectual mother
had to fathom patterns
and pinking sheers,
to cut, press, and transform
her scintillating punning power
into a predictable accuracy of even stitches.

Of Being Poor

My father used to tell me of being poor,
of scrounging carrots for dinner,
this way a wickedness comes,
and the mean ones wear brown robes.
He told me his fingers throbbed
from trying to peel the carrots' thick skins with his boy
fingers.
All his life a blackness under his nails,
his fingers bent and gnarled.
This way a wickedness comes.

Virginia Woolf Without Herself

It was to be without herself.
Not in the old-fashioned sense.
It was to be of fins and pageants.
Feasts and banquets of nameless
villagers and fins afar, swooping
up and down, round and round,
her lust for the journey,
the getting there without time
beyond the horizon in this new
drama. Not to write to name what
there was but to find
what she was without her.

How Your Voice Was

A poem of kindness
How your voice was soft,
Soft as a moth flying
Soft as skin touching new.
How your voice was gentle
Almost a whisper, *hey mister…*
You were so sweetly sure
Of what you knew,
Sleek swordfish certain.
Your soft mouth touched the world
Without a mask, with kindness.
It was then and always only you.

Uncle Sasha

Dear Sasha. Great Sasha.
You were something very special.
In Moscow's somber streets, flagellated
and smothered by summer's heat
and simmering peat bog fires,
you in that outrageously dignified hat
and cane, sickness pushing your bones,
overcame these pains and your daughter's
shame of you to cut a swathe of finesse.

Haunted man who knew prison.
Proud man whose family split and fissured,
warred in the expected Russian-Jewish way.
Sick man just three days out of bed.
I'd watch you as patriarch at your end
of all the tables heavy with food and talk.
You barely had the energy to smile sometimes
but you did and lectured about smoking
through all-conveying looks
of emotion when you caught our eyes.
My grandmother grew red from the efforts
of translation.
I babbled in smiles while the women
stroked and rubbed the top of my head.
I felt a volcano in you.
A bursting open in the long gray hair.

There.
Two worlds barely touching in the air:
American blue jeans. Chekhov in English
My Darling Clementine Slavicized on a dusty victrola.
You'd look at me, the youngest,
wanting and getting something
but all my claims, living in Spain,
the bases, were wanting.

My mother's birthday dinner night
on the 25 floor of Moscow's swankiest hotel
I read the speech you wrote
in English the whole afternoon long
and you stood up speaking in Russian,
saying things that made all the relatives cry,
the agility of Fred Astaire in your body's texture,
the weight of a visionary in your eye.
And I felt an inexperienced pride in family,
the inherited forms.

Dead of pneumonia and gone–
you fused so much and played so lonesome
light, so honor driven.
Man who knew pogroms and the family's
leaving you and war and jail and revolution.

Uncle who said my name like I used to
as a little girl, *Yinda, Yinda.*
I didn't get enough of you.

She Knew Love

Dear Gloria Brim Beckerman Stamler,
Death is a thrush of stop
A brush of heart-wings
My aunt used to say *to be continued*
Because she knew love has no end.
And death shrinks out into a line,
Dissolves our edges into white air.
Oh what we were, how we shone:
Coaligned, conjoined and condoned.
You were a force of nature, an impulse
Under the hurricane, a thrashing of life
Energy, a light that continues
Beyond what we say we are to continue
On into that holy brush of heart-wings–
A nebula of always to be continued, always.

for Molly Neveau

autumn as beginning again

we had a moment of fall radiance today,
the kind of glory Robert Burns
illuminated and framed with bursts of
light and song: an autumnal inverse
of a summer spread of sun
shining tiptoeing now through leaves,
as we watched this miracle settling,
as we talked without talking of
being born again to life.
ourselves free and loose in the sky's airs.
autumn is not an easy ending.
but an affirmation of what we can be
in the trees and the dappled sun,
shining our course clear and gigantic
again.

After the Heart Attack

Sometimes I drive myself crazy
imagining your blood, those silent red rivers.
Sometimes I'd like to go right through your skin
and know for sure that no jagged rocks
mar its even flow, that your channels
are wide and clear and clean, fit
for any worthy boat to sail away and go.
I would vacuum clean those veins for you.
I would build you dikes of polished stone.
But I can't come in.

You're no toy doll
I can ever pull apart and know.
Your big heart beats behind awareness,
a thing no blood test can ever show.
For we sleep with faith, wake to a mystery
again and again and then pull words from us
like clams from reluctant shells,
spooning cold litanies of sound into morning streets.
I fear that no two hearts can ever meet.

But I would see you beat
those gray gamblers at their actuarial games
to live on beyond them,
to move across dying
like sunspots slither over the sun,
I would hear you sing in the bathroom
and watch you go at night to walk alone
and wake to take you to me,

to press that impermeable skin to me,
to lie curled up in a prosperous silence
where we can rock and share and smell
where we can warble a few of our offbeat tunes
until the underground rivers run wild
and put a stop to our splendid show.

Rembrandt goes so deep into the mysterious
that he says things for which there
are no words in any language.
It is with justice that they call
Rembrandt – magician
Vincent Van Gogh

Rembrandt

In his stunning abstract
Dutch-born black,
of what not. Its power,
swarming through enigma
etching the world
with nearly obscene clarity
how gone am I
now in this slippery stone
I would tease life with
your special haunting collars
and live aways here, for to
mingle motley like you do master-
staggered, pruned and flaunted,
I love you, Rembrandt.

To Buck and Linda

Standing Out in the Straight

Haunts of people intense in spring light,
Straw fields and thatched roofs,
Wood fences standing at a slant.
The strangeness of people surge.
Your pale hat whiter than the hills and the sand.
The white of uniqueness. An unsullied tone.
Like you were, holding on to my red shirt
Your body planted firm in my mind–
Woody Herman swinging with Django Reinhardt.
Soulful on syncopated. In that strange balance
We made, standing out in the straight.

This image brought alive the poem
"Standing Out in the Straight" and the cover of this book.

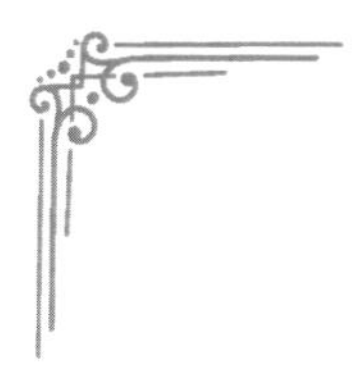

Words

But words do not live in
Dictionaries, they live in the mind

–Virginia Woolf

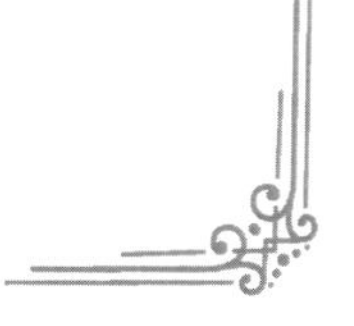

Do not quench your inspiration
and your imagination; do not
become the slave of your model.
Vincent Van Gogh

Poems are for Dancing Minds

Now when I start to write
I want to see it all twisting and turning,
want to see the shape of the words
in the line, want to hear voices talking,
as though a poem could bring to life
thoughts in a painting, could lace
Benjy-like thought.

Poems are not a flat cage
Poems are for dancing minds
that go through the lines
in the most unexpected times.
Italics to mark a new level
Line breaks going on.
Poems are visual, aural, and spacial,
as Wallace Stevens put it:
"the poem of the act of the mind."

Always go too far, because
that's where you'll find the truth.
Albert Camus

Shore Lines in the Sand

Why would I want to write about flat fields
And bright color, to suggest limits and consequence
Why would I want to make pictures
As though I were an artist copying the wind
As though things could be anything
As though there could be shore lines in the sand

As though Camus could ever live without light
As though Cézanne would not paint his canvas thicker and thicker
As though birds lead photographable lives on their perches
Bobbing up on demand to entertain white-faced children
When, backstage, birds beak their worlds bloody
Batter and rush the air in hypnotic trance.

Life is no transparent stillness
with the hollow grace of imaginary holiday.
The forces of flat tussle with the agitations of circumstance.

I want my poems to touch that surge,
that place where blood first moves into sleep,
where heart spears memory as it gropes into time.
I want the crash of titans, life in the round,
to be in the brunt of it,
inside the thunder before the storms,
I want to sustain the bang in the beginning.
Hot headed and sure fired,

poems spin far from flat fields,
to hover inside time and knowing
with the blinding precision of dreams.

Writing in Place

It's about weighing things,
It's about equals,
like to like, peach to peach,
swimming out loud in the ocean
and floating even in the tides
It's about writing in place,
like fitting right into your skin,
heart speech in morning sleep,
writing word for word on the air.
It's like exactly.

Blue cats in the clouds.
It's like nothing extra…
the orange white under the rind there,
that long-clean sweet and fresh,
or Samuel Beckett unwording
the world playing his flute magical.
It's about holding some rhythm
in a groove, sharps folding into flat…
at last Etta James and life is all in the song
like Leslie Howard dancing his elegant face
and Humphrey Bogart gliding through his silhouettes.

It's about writing in place,
here where here is,
this balance, ripe sweet corn cobbing,
wild geese gandering
This sheer sun light
when somehow

you can be as never before
standing out still with yourself
writing in your place
beyond all the words and kissing the sky.

without a signifier in my heart

words words words
as when harmonicas and
Bo Jangles and harpsichords
as when my life goes down
as when flowers pop
as when words fail me
as when it's all translation
as when honeysuckle isn't
honey and words don't say
as when signifiers fall away

Let me sit here forever with bare things.
Things in themselves. Myself being myself.
Virginia Woolf

Dream Language

In this pure silence
where I cannot seem
to say the words by heart
out of my sleep
words that come together in groups
to settle in those floating leaf piles.
Words of my restless mind
becoming suddenly tactile
testing a dream language
turning words inside out in the moment
this language holds on hard
to the bark outside
twisted there in lonely starkness.
It is quiet everywhere here,
so quiet that my lips
flutter and seem to tilt
about in some reserved turmoil.

In this dream language
words are writ large:
images spelling out
the life of living
for us to know by
They come together big
in this image writ to large touching.

They open out all that they are to know
Blossoms red and stray in the bush
My hands sisters in their skin-
The double joints, the familiar bending.
Simple movements. Simple showing.

Things are as they are to be
Open this day in this silence
in a language become physical
like in dreams things are as they are to be.
Blossoms red and stray bits
there hanging on the bush.
Suddenly, nudging the quiet,
a small plane
comes in overhead,
fishing these obscure sunset skies
with a peaceful plainness.

I Want to Read Books

I want to read books that
live in the air, that turn colors
into permanent shrines as Cather and Carver
each commute our psychological entrapments
into shapes of blue boats and white clothes
flapping in a midsummer breeze.
It is to say
I want to hold
on to something so that words
are not what I have to use
when I talk to you
but beacons and lifejackets
in the rage of the line,
the ripple of the moment
when everything goes on through
and into each other.
Writing is our shrine to live by,
to learn from, to shine for.

Poetry: Just This Wonder

Dylan Thomas wedded spatters
of water on leaves to his lingering eye.
He let himself soar and more
so that we felt closer, a kind of
spirit prayer in soft sound.
Hopkins danced through physics
and gave us living metaphysics to
love on: *Márgarét, áre you*
gríeving?.... Rage, rage against the dying of the light.
Poetry is a seamless personification
after all. It turns life inside out
in a spray of words and syllables.
As Louise Glück knew of this unearthly meeting,
the soul creeps out of the tree.
Poetry is just this challenge, this wonder.

I Want Something Gentler

I said out loud, *I want something gentler,*
To the lean afternoon, hearing me say to myself
Gentler. Rows of bookshelves in Bilbao
Throbbed a dusty yes. With a happy sureness
Of baffled old stars. It was as though
Time was perhaps threading something harsh.
And here I was in this cascading fall sunlit
Afternoon threshing myself to make safety.
I'm beyond bohemian finding now.
Now the making is now all on me, to make gentler,
To thread the nuances in a green sled of harmony
Linda-stitched and driven to make my way now
On my own, gentler and somehow sweeter in sunlit air.

Beginnings

Never start a poem with the word *the.*
Starfish will fly blind-eyed
And scatter like old finches
In soft wet sand
Overwhelmingly
A poem writes to become:
Writes to find in language
A pale flag in a new dark
A banister beginning

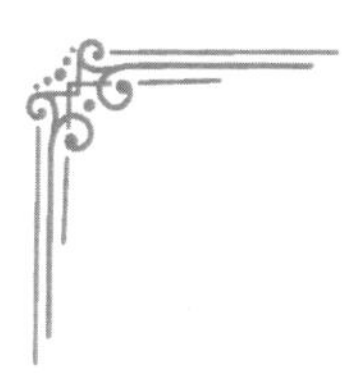

Places

To walk through a landscape is to walk through a culture,
for it is culture that determines both what we are
and what a landscape is for us

–David Hinton

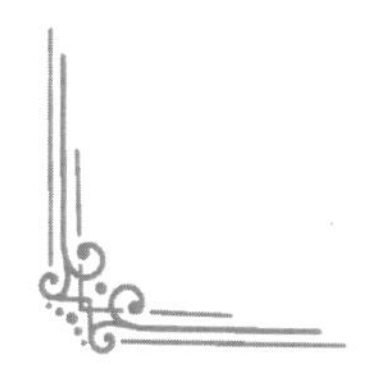

In the American West

In the center of the American West,
space is the etiquette for love
and mountains the reed playing infinity.
Standing tall, there, while the
transcendental
universe sweeps its wind,
spreads that completeness.

World as a Terror-Field

Think of those sunflower petals
Flying away so yellow in a golden light
Think of the anarchists' red shirts
Pungent in Guadalajara, overt and blood-drenched
Think of you this sunny morning receiving a spam email
Threatening to contaminate your whole house.
There is no safe place anymore to dream of La La Land.
We can be reached anywhere and pulled and tugged,
Unhinged even from the safety of our soul.
I think of Virginia Woolf having coffee, her mind,
Measuring the world of decades, stirring the sugar in her coffee.
It's as though her mind-place reached around the world.
At a glance, with her word nest intact.
Now, we are within walls polished so transparent
Our souls close like an x-ray's light, all seen into.
There's a terror of no intimacy,
leaking passwords and invasive viruses.
Curse those who disparage the robin
Plucking away, the stalwart bluejay.
Curse those who say we don't matter
Anyway, any way.

Hot California Morning

Hot California morning. Among great
trees we were like children pine needle
stepping. We walked fine in time waiting
there for it to happen in absolute quiet.
Life was among a rustling. Bird hops and
crow caws.
Everything was. We were playing catch-up.
Breathing softly. Wondering like stars.
In this high-heat stillness, with cracking
and occasional brown bears. It was
as though it all just began.
In the miracle pine needles we were
stepping in. Trees at the top,
needling and kneading the sky.

A Semiotic Silence

The music is silent here
snow nears bringing
semiotic silence, a wordless cooing
of late beginners.
When we were young
getting high,
it seemed
we said everything without
crickets or sound even.
It was, then, so simple, it seemed,
to explain everything---
whereas, now clouds claw sight
and words fail, flat falling
without belief to sing us.
And we must be as nightingales
to sing louder, to ring us out.

When the Tourists Are Gone

How far from the common ideas of Spain,
a land of wine and castles and castanets
are the fading streets of any secondary town
and its drudgery of iron-barred windows.
It's banks and bars and babies
where scrawny dogs limp in the dirt for food.
It's tiny dim-lit neighborhood stores
where crowds of gigantic women rub behinds
and dead cats rot untouched in the alleys.
It's broken glass and garbage and uniforms
of soldiers, children and the roundelay
of ladies dragging their carts to market every day.
It's trudge and drudge and doubtful hopes.
Blind lottery vendors sell tickets in the dark,
buttons missing on a gray-stained coat.

It's two jobs daily and a quart of beer.
The sun's no object. It's an unforgetting witness
here to these ghost town streets
where when the tourists are gone in winter
the buildings look like barracks
and the things of this world keep running
into one another in a dissonant way
as though the loss of them and their glitter
made less of hope. It's back to beans
again and sweaters and cold in the bones.
It's back to the houses, those empty shells
are overcrowded, overheated rooms of stone.
Subject now to the skies whimsey

the heart, that famous southern fire, hibernates
and sheds the exotic skins of summer
in this most Arabic part of Spain
where it will rain and rain
washing the streets clean of its leavings
and the envy tourists have sown
in order to take pride in Christmas
and the people can make the un-equivocating streets
completely, though bitterly, again
their own.

This Way and That

in the shade outside
the shadow of late
summer moving
the trees around
out there as a stranger
pulling hoses would
she thinks of herself
once in a greener grass
in the leaves like a woman
moving this way and that
this way and then
feeling it all together
fitting and meeting
she thinks of herself
as she remembers herself
dancing on a rooftop
her body giddy in the moonlight

How Where We Lived Was

On the street where you lived.
We bought a house without the roots
you hated those false forever knots
and wanted to keep us stars in the trees
on the street where we lived
you made mulch and turned honey golden
and I surrounded us with flowers
and dried the herbs and seasonings of our summers.

Where we were, there, complete, in a love beyond the saying
as a music of smoky sounds, tenor sax bleeding
the whole tones of us making a love beyond words
for to say what I loved about your face.
Holiday birds we thrived in a green room.
Half-moons rising in our eyes
sudden like solid smoke. On that street where we lived
together like stars in the trees. Such a singing without song-sound.

Two refugees planting each other fresh in the air,
a hoe-line could have not sown them any surer.
Strange star roots in the open. Once you said we
knew paradise. Just like that. A paradise. Star roots we were
surely, free to spread about with the honey and those roses.

On the Town to Talk Color

Our feet crunched the stones
in Tours, an echo sound, we were
on the town to talk color,
yes, to see how color was,
all of us writing light in the air,
we looked at each other as
though we'd just been born
our umbilical cords sliding away.
We had everything to learn,
everything to see, crunching
along, crunching to help our steps
stay a bit brighter and longer.

To Be A Pilgrim

How wide the street light was.
We felt like pilgrims
there in San Francisco: poets–
notebooks in hand
and painters and revolutionaries
feeling freedom touching a new world.
We dressed in velvet purple:
regal in mind and body.
How lovely it was;
To be a pilgrim that way.

It might appear that nothing is
happening, but that's actually when
it really happens.
Keith Richards

Sand on the Beach

That noon. The sand. Spread as a piece of skin.
It lay there new. Small bulges rounding.
It spread and spread
like reading Don Quixote in Spain,
in sentences that spread like silk sounding.
The vowels sheer predicates of nuance unfolding.
Time and nouns shared a space of a mind coming to know,
coming to know how everything.
Floated like the skin inside your thigh with nameless softness,
namelessly soft like gums are,
like you could tell the truth on it in it.
And as I looked in the sand I saw the seas of my life
drifting flowing on by, soundless
and I knew then with the skin-soft sand
that my only job ever would be to come to name it all softly,
namelessly soft in nameless wonder like the sand spreading
like skin in noon light.

Considerations

On a hill being questioned here as to how to live
How would I ever know when I can barely walk

Linda Chown

Kind of Floating

As I recall all of these twenty years.
Kind of floating. All those books
I read in 3-D depth, intricacies flying
as I became myself finding their wings
and it was all so genuine,
texts sticking together, words standing up
and now I'm looming over myself
roaming and learning how long
beauty stays. Ronnie Wood and
the plethora of the Straits of Gibraltar.
All my friends always I love you.
As I grow without my voice
I can touch the ocean,
feel the pine sounds,
and love life deliberatively.

Saying nothing...
Sometimes says the most
Emily Dickinson

A Silent Way to Say

When I was young and shy,
there was a silent way to say,
a way of making life
larger and doubling
what you knew
twiddling your thumbs like
you did little that you were.
I fled from the talkers,
the word mongers, and punners saying too much.
I fled into silence to go into touch.

Is it not the play of the mind we
are after? Is it not that that shows
a mind is there at all?
Charles Olson

How Sarah Saw to Herself

At night in a quiet room,
she sank deep into the lights of dreaming,
to hold on to what she was
finding out about seeing colors,
nuances shaping up in the night.
Her always wide eyes. Wheezes
knocking at the doors of her chest,
like shutters flapping in a Texas wind.
The decisive whack of wood.
Even when nobody heard her
hear to say the fabric of what
she was coming to know to think.
When she was all locked up little
in those taffeta clothes,
tiny buttons and plackets,
tight around her. When she was bending
her toes around, wriggling them, just to tell
how she saw to herself.
To remember the smooth spots
that she knew she knew by heart,
but only when she was alone
those times fitting into herself,
while she was in the corner
coming to settle into herself.

Just knowing how she was
in that light of hers darkly,
paddling the peeling moments like a sailor
and starching the intricate fibers of memory
with near collarbone precision.
Her voice, a feather of tulips in the morning.

poetry is not simple

It pains me that
poetry is not
simple
today grief is
complex
overcome by names
to try to know
it by.
It pains me that
poetry is not
simple
give me a coffee cup
a blue door
your oblong hat:
give me
a range of simple.

And the rain is brain-colored
Stan Rice

Brain Drops

And, suddenly, the street people
on fire, their bone-backs arch,
stretching into cold air,
like orange live wires
broiling the night
wet.

Fervent spectacle of brain drops,
sky-scapes of spider writing,
Burnt alchemies curving in.
Sheets of golden marrow
hover, spinning
perpendicular.

Translucent sparks
of brain paste flicker
splendid tawny--
writing rain articulate across urgent sky.

Yet I have a soul, Mrs. Jarvis would bethink her…
Virginia Woolf

Bethinking

She rode on a think,
rode ramshackle light,
her airs thoroughly whip-poor-will.
It was first all about the sweep,
so sweet and steep.
Bethinking herself
she went all in, heading
her all widewelter
through the tide.
Learning to spin still to
foreshadow before when.
Riding her think warpwise,
rotating light, wedgeward
through long straits of angle,
spinning ramshackle light
where the whip-poor-wills will.

A Place For Sorrow

Grief and gratitude
like a horse and sparrow
feed feeling into the right place.
Ashes and barley with
acorns and beetroot.
There's a way to make
a new feeling, one that
grows profuse color in
wallowing wisdom.

There is no use for sorrow
where the sun goes down
the roots will be rising,
maples all leafing,
and you seeding your life
plentiful.

All the Way For Love

Going all the way for love
never leaves. Your skin glows
and grows more intricately you. It's
as though once loved, your fibers
change
your soul an epiphany made
physical.
Inside, this cooing.

The Breath of My Blood

These two years
Have thickened me, left me bewildered,
High and dry as the debris in an elephant's eye,
Ringing unanswered bells in white hell halls.
How I wanted to run again
And to seem determined.
How the breath of my blood
Stiffened and I came to
Look nice without my old exotic,
That fire in a thin emphatic face,
Those lingering lips and know it all eyes,
How my feet grow restlessly stiff
How I sleep with oxygen
How I have gotten permanently
Sick dramatically and unrecoverably smitten.

Questions Around the Lake

Afternoon storms roiling at the Cloisters
Make me think of Wallace Stevens walking
Slowly around the lake and the flowers
Floating remind me of Jesus and the aftermath
On a hill being questioned over and over,
Big men with round black glasses
Urge me to answer them
As to how I live now, how to cast my stones
How to live urgent in my used bones
How to target the median strip
When everyone is dying now it seems
The storms remind me of fir trees fleeting
In California dust. In the earth that made me.
I am a disciple of that beauty. It heals my shambles
On a hill being questioned here as to how to live
How would I ever know when I can barely walk.

And all the lives we ever lived and all the lives to be
Are full of trees and changing leaves
Virginia Woolf

Holding onto it now

Soft bird, as though we've only just begun,
The way our arms reach upwards, as though
Hanging in a William Blake painting
In which closeness is everything,
The spiritual become all physical.
A radiant yellow cloud of pulsing light
In spite of all the bad light around,
This beauty only makes a luscious sound.
Soft bird, you and I continue to soar
Onward and upwards forever.

Knowing it Strangely

In the spring
reading Ripley's colored
Believe It Or Not books, I thought of
Wonderland and hookahs,
of the ways things go through
each other to the other side.
An eloquent vanishing.
Not just any bell book and candle,
But Kim Novak effervescent on Powell Street.
Elizabeth Taylor shining gold
near where the water was,
near where the mysteries lay uncovered.
Where the swami speaks of transformation
and solid things shiver
bigger.

What tenderness in these little words, what savagery
Samuel Beckett

That Green Sheen

Near the lake, a green sheen
With the perfection of ink, I think roses
And corpses besides the sources–
Your play about today's discourses.
Beckett had this way of touching
What we didn't say what we had before
We could know, like a thin red line,
Like the opining an old maestro
Might attempt at the corner
Of his living, four wheels and scissors.
Words that started like sheep
Neighing unlike themselves.

How wonderful it is that
nobody need wait a single moment
before starting to improve the world.
Anne Frank

Little Girl and the Sailing Moon

It is like how to explain the paucity of beauty
on a hillside, how to hold silence stiller.
Clumps of marjoram, Greek symbol of happiness, make a plenty.
Forthwith in this troubled land where the President of France
was face cuffed, where thousands of sick boys
play murderous games and sing aloud to blood.
How to hold silence stiller to make a plenty.
When I was then her, she held life in this staring.
In the city she saw the moon sail and marjoram
grew while she stood trying to understand Anne Frank,
who was too a little girl staring like she was and going
to feel her roots and her eyes pulverized all dying.
We must hold silence riper and green the marjoram.

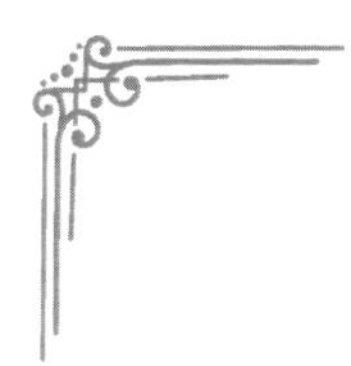

Moments

There is that complete focus in forever,
unexpectedly soft landings in always

Linda Chown

To Richard Marks

August

August we want your excess and daring
But not these sudden losses
Of these brave and beautiful ones
We want the August geniuses
To fill us with the excess we need
To withstand the mundane
To sow disorder and excess
To scatter wild into the same.

A Time For God

This is the time for God,
for a roaring sonorous voice,
a biblical moment, indeed,
when we're shouldering the slaughtered
daily,
trying to assuage the fire of fear in and
around us,
when leaders spring forth and speak
with the hallowed tone of the ancient
tabernacle.
Ages old salt smells, a smear of blood–
We're ready for the divine, dying alive in our
concern. This big, larger than life moment
when life and death waver voluptuously
around us.

November 22, 1963

It was to be in
History like a fold
Folding, the world clipped
At the end of reality marks
Where we were joined
In a terribly sudden way
On the day of Dallas bullets
In Berkeley it was all sunny
As we felt history like a fold
Wrapping us in a bloody knoll
As we stood long the world
Clipped us into the moment
At the end of old reality laid
Bare there where we were
Manifolded in history.

Death Into This Spring

Spring finds us speechless
to say, to say how terror is,
how death turns our head.
We've been used to letting life
go by without us.
I breathe hard for life with addled lungs.
After all, we are life, all there is of it.
Now in the heart of growth,
death is climbing hard
toward us all over.
Now, we have to stand out in the balance
and ring our life for living,
jump and plunge
over the edge into what comes next.
Quick the blue iris is coming
and the red peonies
and all your wonderful life.

A March 2022 Poem With War

When it is a world of hats…
fedora, bowler, cloche, beret–
we have a layer of disguise,
like we had all the big words
undercover to show ourselves with:
sanguinary libidinous languid–
like today the words explode
a way into verbal regiments,
soundless lines of names.
I disappears into lingual turbans.
The streets bombed meanwhile
beyond sleep, mottled and
thrust into violent silence.
Eerie-long mirror images
of death dying. This fog of what
what is not under the hat or
beyond the horizon anywhere.

We struggle under the brim.

Christopher Columbus was said to be
captivated in 1492 by a faint light
"like the light of a wax candle moving
up and down" in the water

The Burning of The Sea

The sea seems to burn all over
With enchanted light,
Almost a soundful of glimmers
Which glow without burst
And time keeps on shining
As your heart burns with love.
You look astounded
At an ordinary miracle
Happening right here
Then, when time hovered
Burning with us at twilight,
Movement turned space over
In Bergsonian slow motion
Turning divine in shallow waters.

when your memory

when your memory
gets too big to see with,
when then and now get
snarled and twisted,
a kind of thicket
just remember your childhood fires,
those darting shapes with no names,
just redness, and that snapping in
a sudden swirl and you were close
and memory an untangled vine.

An absolute can only be given in an intuition,
Henri Bergson

White Sound

There is this dignity in time
open and without measure really,
shore paddies swelling,
white syncopated sound.
Light fables drift inbound,
myth-bright in epic moment.

There is that complete focus in forever,
unexpectedly soft landings in always.
Pure cobbled luminescence
where matter pools into volume,
when energy is saturating velocity
and time curves along into stillness.

But hurry, let's entwine ourselves as one,
our mouth broken, our soul bitten by love,
so time discovers us safely destroyed.
Federico García Lorca

Sunfishing

Lorca knew death rises
That death thrusts its blood
How the lonely bestow heart-speak
Wicked white clouds cloud La Plaza de Toros
Where death spears life dreams
And the sun spitfishes your skin
Over time you will ask for many
Promises from the wrong ones
But Lorca knows that death rises in the high times of the tarde
Kiss me sweetheart one lip by one
Let us fish sun together
As we always have done.

Linda's Whitmore paradise.

Whitmore's gardens.

Cobblestones in Cádiz.

Two señoras hanging out.

Three widows behind closed windows.

Conil de la frontera, en Andalucía.

Anne Rice, Miriam (Linda's mother), Linda and Jennifer at a party at the Rice's.

Rhoney Stanley (middle back), Jennifer (left), Rhoney's son (middle forward), Linda (right).

(From left to right) Buck, Juan Gonzáles, Linda, and Juan's son.

(left to right) Besse Brim, Linda, and Aunt Anita in Leningrad.

Jennifer holding little Rina.

Rina and Jennifer.

Mother's day celebration with Miriam, Jennifer, Rina, and Linda.

A sisterly look between Linda and Jennifer.

Linda's lovely niece Rina.

Sunlitwoman

Jennifer, Linda, and Abbi

Sunfishing

Acknowledgements

To Buck Hosman, my love always.

My list to be complete would be hundreds of names, specific great poems and physical places. California, Seattle, and across the Pacific Ocean, seventeen years teaching and living in Spain, and in northern London.

To my parents and grandparents, and to Gloria who always showed me their love. They each gave me confidence and the impetus to reach and be more.

To Leigh Eicke, Abigail Best, and Karisha Diaz who taught me in individual ways how to try to be excellent in spite of whatever life throws your way.

For Kirsty Gunn who believed in me and taught me how writing can be both magic and truth.

Citations

The Bardo Group Beguines
"A Time for God" June 23, 2020

> A special huge thanks to my close friend Jamie Dedes for her support and love. Many thanks for your commitment to my Blake series. For you, I hope to publish them one day.
> https://thebezine.com/author/intothebardo/

The BeZine March 15, 2022
"I Want to Read Books"
"Knowing It Strangely" appears in the BeZine as "On the Other Side of Things"

The BeZine December, 2021
"How Sarah Saw to Herself"
"Sand on the Beach"
"Beginnings"

> Applause is due to Michael Dickel for his commitment to the just life, his knowledge of world literature, and his interest in and defense of poetry.
> https://thebezine.com/

Meat for Tea: The River Valley Review Volume 16, Issue 1.
March, 2022
Russian Caravan issue
"Uncle Sasha,"
"My Mother Had A Scar, "
"August The Day After."

Meat for Tea: The River Valley Review Raw Issue Volume 15, Issue 4, December, 2021.
"Questions Around the Lake,"
"Intense Little Girl,"
"Beginnings."

Many thanks to Elizabeth MacDuffie for her editorial excellence, support of these poems, and her important defense of the term "*Aesthetic.*"
Http://meatfortea.com

Poethead October 8, 2016
"Shore-lines in the Sand"
"Writing in Place"
Epigraph to this book

Deep thanks and respect to the splendid writer and artist Chris Murray who years ago asked me for my poems in ***Poethead***. Her commitment to women writers is a powerful support.
https://poethead.wordpress.com/2016/10/08/doris-lessing-said-i-was-a-child-of-violence-and-other-poems-by-linda-chown/

Linda Chown Bio

Born in Berkeley, California, Linda Chown has lived in England, Spain, California, and Seattle, Washington. She's gotten used to spectacular beauty and a plethora of breathtaking cultural places. As a professor of American, Comparative, and Women's Literatures, and a leader at the Poetry Center at San Francisco State University in the 1960s, she has known a wide swath of artists, leaders, and political characters in her active life. She has grown to admire and study the work of introspective writers like William Butler Yeats, Virginia Woolf, Katherine Mansfield and William Faulkner, whose writing, like her own, passionately reconsiders and renames their realities.

Scholar, researcher, and writer, she has written all her life. Ever active, she published four books of poetry, a stream of reviews, poems, and prose overviews of writers, as well as a study comparing narration in writers Carmen Martín Gaite and Doris Lessing. In this book, she suggests new terms and concepts for reading prose.

Over time, she went from the sunny streets of the Haight Ashberry to the towers of Oxford Street in London and the sun-drenched beaches of the Playa Victoria in Cádiz to a quiet large house overlooking a ravine in Grand Rapids, Michigan. Overall, she is committed to being different, to non-dogmatic writing and living, ever learning it new. Decades of teaching taught her to cherish classroom moments in which the walls and barriers become transparent. She loves this holy closeness.

Made in the USA
Middletown, DE
24 February 2024

50279706R00058